THE
KINGDOM
OF
WHITE
WATERS

THE
KINGDOM
OF
WHITE
WATERS

A SECRET STORY

Radiant Books
New York

The Kingdom of White Waters was originally written in Russian in 1893 by V.G. who wished to remain anonymous. Translated from the Russian by Alexander Gerasimchuk with John Woodsworth, Member of the Literary Translators' Association of Canada.

Published in 2022 by Radiant Books
radiantbooks.co

ISBN 978-1-63994-027-1 (paperback)
ISBN 978-1-63994-026-4 (e-book)

CONTENTS

HOW THIS STORY WAS WRITTEN

On 12 July 1893, I arrived with my three younger brothers in the Dormition Monastery of Vysha, Tambov Governorate, about 65 kilometres distant from the village of Zemetchino where we lived. This monastery was founded in 1625, being located at the mouth of the Vysha river, on its left bank. It is especially well known for its miraculous Mother-of-God icon.

At the monastery we were greeted very warmly, like old friends, for we had already been there — back in the summer of 1890 for a one-week stay. Besides, they treated us more than cordially, as they respected our father for his love of the monastery, his sincere faith, sacrifice, and repeated help to the monastery with both advice and practical support.

While visiting the Father Superior, I asked him, among other things, to give me the opportunity to talk with one of the well-read monks who could help me resolve a number of questions that had arisen from reading the Gospel, as well as from daily life.

"For example, what kind of questions might you be interested in?" the abbot asked.

To this I mentioned two questions that I had asked a vast multitude of people countless times, yet had never received, to my understanding, a satisfying answer.

"Firstly, while not doubting that the power emanating from Christ Jesus healed a woman suffering from bleeding, awakened the dead, cast out demons, and healed the sick, I would like to know if there is mentioned somewhere in the lives of the saints, who also performed many miracles, something in more detail about this divine power?"

The Father Superior replied: "Everything is possible for the Lord God and His ways are inscrutable; the more sincerely we believe, the happier we shall be."

To this I, in turn, responded: "In the Gospel is it said: 'Ask, and it shall be given to you; knock, and it shall be opened unto you'; therefore, I really desire to speak with a spiritually well-read and developed person who could give me the explanations I'm looking for.

"Secondly, how is it possible to explain that in 1885 the hieromonk accompanying the miraculous icon of the Vysha Mother-of-God predicted to my mother that her prayer was heard by the Lady and her wish would be fulfilled — which, indeed, happened eighteen months later. My mother asked to grace her with a daughter — and she was born."

To this the abbot said: "To monks and people with rich spiritual understanding, the Divine Forces reveal much more than to others."

Then the abbot, after talking about the beauty of spiritual life, spoke to me like a father and said that he would give me the opportunity to converse with a very well-read monk. Still, for the sake of my spiritual interests, he would like me to believe more and reason less.

Following the evening service, a novice came up to me, saying that after supper he would take me to see Hieromonk Vladimir, who wanted to converse with me.

The hieromonk greeted me very cordially. Our two-hour conversation simply flew by.

The next day was 15 July, the name-day of our Saint Vladimir. After the prayer service, we met again. Among other questions, I asked him whether he happened to know the legend of the Grail Castle and how should it be understood. To this, Hieromonk Vladimir replied that this legend of the Western peoples is interesting and instructive and that, like many other legends, it had its own foundation, concealing a profound meaning. This legend, like most others, was expounded symbolically and was accessible to everyone's comprehension, depending on their spiritual understanding.

Then I asked: "Do you happen to know of any similar legend among our people?"

After a while, Hieromonk Vladimir replied: "I don't know any legend, but I was personally entrusted with a certain ancient and secret story of *Belovodye* ["The Land of White Waters"], which I could, in some way, in a spiritual sense, compare to this legend, despite the outward seeming difference of plots."

I very much wanted him to tell me this narrative, but Hieromonk Vladimir was silent. Feeling in my soul that some kind of doubt had arisen in him, and seeing that he still did not answer, I did not hesitate to repeat my request, adding: "If the knowledge of the story entails some other requirement, then I promise in advance to fulfil it."

To this, Hieromonk Vladimir answered: "You are the first person to ask me to tell them this story. I feel that you are an especially lucky man. I can entrust it to you, knowing that you will observe the condition of the vow of silence. You have the right to retell this story for the first time only to someone who asks you repeatedly about it. After that, your vow of silence will no longer be in force. However, this will not happen soon. At that time, you will probably be older than I am! As a matter of fact, I have now just turned 61 years old.

"Until then, you yourself must not tell it to anyone of your own free will — they will not understand you and it will be hard for you. Nevertheless, in the future, its meaning will be accessible only to rare people, too.

"This evening, let's go to the pine forest — it is more fitting there, in spacious surroundings, to touch upon the exalted questions which your soul strives to understand but is yet unable to fully embrace — in view of your still insufficiently developed consciousness."

In the evening after supper, taking with me a pencil and a notebook, I met with Hieromonk Vladimir. After a few minutes of walking, we found ourselves in a wonderful forest surrounding the monastery.

Taking a seat on a stump, Hieromonk Vladimir began his narrative. After asking his permission, I began writing it down verbatim.

Hieromonk Vladimir would sometimes get up, walk around a bit, and then sit down again. After dictating several sentences, he at the same time expressed his own views and responded to my questions.

He told me that the story was entrusted to him some thirty years ago, at the last confession, by an elderly monk. And he, in turn, could pass it on, but only to one who asked him for it. Otherwise, he was obliged to recount the story to his confessor for the 28th time (counting from the very beginning), only upon feeling the approach of death.

He revived the story many times in his memory, attempting to follow and walk the path described in it, and dared to imagine himself in the place of Father Sergius. At the same time, he always felt a pleasant spiritual thrill, sometimes even wondrous feelings bordering on bliss while time kept passing unnoticed.

When it started to get dark, we stopped writing. I gave Hieromonk Vladimir what I had written with a request to check it carefully.

On the third evening, the work was completed.

Continuing to converse with Hieromonk Vladimir in the evenings, I stayed at the monastery for several more days.

After sincerely thanking Hieromonk Vladimir for the wonderful, unforgettable hours of conversation, and upon receiving his blessing with a feeling of great gratification, I left the hospitable abode happy and contented.

V.G.
November 1893
Village of Zemetchino,
Tambov Governorate,
Morshansk Uyezd

In later life, during conversations, it seemed that the question of Belovodye did not arouse any interest in my interlocutors. Exactly half a century has passed imperceptibly and I will soon be 65 years old.

On 28 July 1943, at the Ciechocinek resort, Poland, for the first time, I met a person who, in a conversation with me, asked whether I knew anything about Belovodye, about whose existence he had heard, yet, despite his best efforts, could learn nothing more from anyone. This was a famous Russian folk poet and psaltery player — Alexander Efimovich Kotomkin, whose name, with his consent, is given here.

Upon learning that I had a story, he was very happy and earnestly asked me to convey it to him — which I did. Thus Hieromonk Vladimir's foresight came true.

The vow of silence has now been removed from me and the story becomes the heritage of the peoples of the Earth, for the designated period has come and the New Time is upon us.

V.G.
28 June 1943
Ciechocinek resort,
near the right bank of
the Vistula river in Poland

The Secret Story of Belovodye was published for the first time in *Novaya Zarya* [New Dawn], a Russian daily newspaper issued in San Francisco, California (in the Easter issue No. 5109, 24 April 1949, pp. 12–14).

THE
SECRET
STORY
OF
BELOVODYE

Recorded on 15 July 1893 from the words of Father Vladimir, a hieromonk of the Dormition Monastery of Vysha, Tambov Governorate, Shatsky Uyezd.

I

In his desire to change the faith, Grand Prince Vladimir the Red Sun, a wise ruler of Kievan Rus,* sent six richly appointed embassies to foreign lands to investigate what faiths were there. Then, upon comparing them, he planned to choose the best one for himself and all his people.

Shortly after seeing off the embassies, a wanderer approached the Grand Prince. It was Father Sergius, who at a young age had journeyed together with some tradespeople from Kiev to Constantinople. He was converted to Christianity on the Holy Mount Athos, and took monastic vows. After staying there

---

* Kievan Rus (862–1242) was the first East Slavic state formed around the city of Kiev, the seat of the Grand Prince. It included most of present-day Ukraine and Belarus and part of northwest Russia.

until the age of thirty, he returned home. Since the world had not understood him and he could not walk together with the world, he did not want to have a specific place of residence. Preoccupied with introspection and contemplation of the soul, he wandered all year round across the domains of the Grand Prince, as well as through other nearby lands. Watching how people live, he helped everyone in every way he could, entrusting the light of truth to the worthy and converting them to Christianity. Every three years, Father Sergius came to Kiev and visited the Grand Prince.

Great was the joy of Father Sergius when he learnt about the dispatching of the embassies — especially the fact that one of them was directed to Constantinople, for he was convinced that there was no faith higher than Christianity.

The Grand Prince, too, was glad about his arrival. Yet at the same time he was sad that Father Sergius had not come earlier, for the Prince wanted him in particular to head the embassy to Constantinople.

The Grand Prince also told Father Sergius that many times in dreams an elder had appeared to him, indicating that an additional seventh embassy should be dispatched. But he did not know where to send it, and asked Father Sergius' advice.

After pondering, Father Sergius replied that, since the embassy to Constantinople had already been dispatched, he did not know and was unaware of any other possible destinations. However, the Grand Prince insisted on his own rightness and ordered him to decide within seven days where to send the seventh embassy.

Wishing to help the Grand Prince, Father Sergius began a strict fast and prayerfully requested the Most High to send him a revelation as to what answer to give the Prince.

On the seventh night, in a dream, Father Sergius had a vision of the abbot of the Mount Athos monastery, where he had taken his vows. The abbot reminded him about the ancient legend of Belovodye. Upon awakening, Father Sergius thanked the Lord for the revelation received and distinctly remembered what he had heard from the abbot during his stay in the monastery.

In remote antiquity, a Byzantine king, unhappy with his and his people's faith, summoned sages from all over the country. He asked them to advise him where to send embassies for the purpose of choosing a new and better faith.

After long discussions, one of the sages, who came from the East, said that in his time, his teacher, a wise elder, imparted to him that somewhere in the far Orient there existed a country named *Belovodye* — a fabulous abode of eternal beauty and truth, and this was where he felt they needed to seek advice. However, he mentioned that one of the features of this realm was that not everyone could find, reach, and enter it, but only a chosen one — someone who had been specifically called thereto.

The king liked the legend, and he equipped and dispatched an embassy to the East, led by the sage. After twenty-one summers, the sage returned, but alone — all his companions had died on the journey.

The king listened with delight to the amazing stories of the one who got back. Everything was so good and reasonable that he renounced his faith and, on the advice of the sage, introduced a new one. However, not everything narrated by the wise man was clear: much seemed simply impossible and people made fun of him, believing he was telling tall tales.

Father Sergius conveyed this legend to Grand Prince Vladimir. He was so inspired that he, too, decided to send an embassy to the East, to the unknown country, and put Father Sergius in charge of it.

After much hassle the embassy was put together.

Six people of noble blood were given to Father Sergius as assistants, along with many distinguished warriors and a considerable array of servants. The embassy numbered 333 people in all.

Once the season of high water had passed, the embassy embarked upon its journey to the Orient. It was estimated that it would return in about three years. During the first year regular reports came through the adjacent lands which the embassy crossed on its way to the East. Then all at once everything lapsed into silence. Three, seven, even twelve years passed, yet there was no news of the embassy. At first people waited for it, then they worried about its fate; finally they grieved over the missing. But after twenty-eight years, with still no message forthcoming, they started to forget. And time gradually covered everything.

II

Forty-nine years after that, an elder monk arrived at the city of Kiev together with one of the embassies from Constantinople. After living seven years as a hermit, with a premonition of his impending death, he made a confession, which included a precious secret — a secret that could only be conveyed in person, from mouth to mouth. This innermost story would eventually become the property of the peoples of the Earth on its own, but not until the appointed time — at the dawn of a New Era for humankind.

• • •

I am the monk Father Sergius, who fifty-six years ago was sent with the embassy by Grand Prince Vladimir the Red Sun to search for Belovodye. This is my account of our journey.

During the first year we travelled well. Despite many clashes and crossings, there was little loss of either people or animals. After passing through many different lands and crossing two seas, it became more and more difficult to advance during the second year: people and cattle died, roads became impassable, and we learnt nothing from our enquiries among the locals. People became discontent and grumbled, there being still no sign of our goal in sight.

Towards the end of the second year, our route took us through a desert. The farther we went, the more we came across the skeletons of people, horses, camels, donkeys, and other animals. When we arrived at a large open area which was entirely covered with bones, people refused to go forward.

At a general meeting it was decided that those who wished to turn back might do so; as a result, only two people agreed to go on with me.

By the end of the third year of our journey, first one of my companions, then the other, fell sick. I had to leave them at a settlement.

While caring for the latter fellow, I managed to learn from the chief of this settlement that approximately thirty years ago, another seeker of the Land of Wonders had come through, riding towards the East, accompanied by a caravan of camels. It turned out that a man who had served as a guide for this caravan was still alive, and that he lived but a three days' journey from there. I sent for him, and he agreed to take me further and then to entrust me to another guide, provided he was able to find one.

With successive changes of guides, I made my way slowly forward. One of them told me that, according to legends, wanderers had passed through there even earlier, aiming to find the Secret Land lying to the East. This information heartened me and I fervently prayed to the Lord to lead me further.

After a few more changes of guides, I encountered one who imparted to me what he had learnt from the words of travellers coming from the Orient. According to their accounts, somewhere in the East, about a seventy days' journey away, was situated a wondrous land high in the mountains, which many aspired to reach. But few were able to penetrate it and even fewer returned.

The farther I went, the more information I received. There could be no doubt that the realm I longed to behold actually existed. Some called it the "Forbidden Land," or the "Land of White Waters and High Mountains." Others called it the "Land of Bright Spirits," the "Land of the Living Fire," the "Land of Wonders," or by a variety of other names, all referring to one and the same country.

Finally, we reached a settlement where I was told that the border of the Forbidden Land was but three days distant. A guide would take me as far as the boundary, but would be unable to accompany me further, at the risk of his own life. A few travellers, proceeding on their own, but failing to find any roads, had turned back. On the rare — extremely rare — occasion, a pilgrim might remain and live there for a long time. But rumour had it that anyone else had perished.

After praying, I set out with my final guide.

As the road kept rising, it became narrower and narrower. In some places it was possible for only one person to pass through at a time, and with considerable difficulty at that.

It was not long before we found ourselves surrounded by high mountains with snow-covered peaks.

After a third night's sleep, the guide presently informed me that he could not take me any further.

According to various legends, at a distance of three to seven days' journey, if one kept heading towards the highest visible peak, one might come upon a settlement. Yet very few had ever reached it.

At this point the guide abandoned me, his receding steps fading into the distance.

III

The rising Sun illuminated the snow-white peaks of the mountains, and the reflection of the rays gave the impression that they were enveloped in a fiery flame.

No soul was around. I was alone with my Lord who led me here after such a long journey. Feelings of indescribable happiness, rapture, and ethereal joy overwhelmed me, and at the same time I was conscious of a deep inner peace. I lay down on the pathway with my head directed towards the highest summit, I kissed the stony soil and, while shedding tears of emotion, I was thanking the Lord without words, as best I could, for His Grace.

I proceeded further. Soon there was a crossroad — both pathways, it seemed, led to the highest mountain. I followed the right-hand one, for it was pointing towards the course of the Sun.

I walked forward with a prayer and a song.

On the first day I encountered two more crossroads. At the second of these, I spied a little snake crawling across one of the pathways, as though blocking my way. And so I decided to follow the other trail. At the third intersection, three stones lay across one of the paths. I set off along the free one.

On the second day, there was a fourth crossing, where the pathway I was on forked into three. A butterfly fluttering on one of the paths prompted me to choose it. In the afternoon, my journey took me past a mountain lake. With exaltation and astonishment, I admired its beauty and weightless ripple, which in the prevailing light added an amazing and special whiteness to the waters of the lake.

On my third day of journeying through this land, the rays of the rising Sun once again illumined the snow-white veils of the highest mountain, surrounding it with a fiery flame. My entire soul burst heavenward — I stared and could not feast my eyes enough, the scene was so beautiful. As my lips formed a silent prayer, my soul merged with the flame enveloping the mount. Not letting it out of my sight, I started to notice that this fire became alive: in its streams appeared the figures of Angels. They shone with a dazzling white resplendence, while continuously flying towards the mountain in exquisite roundelays. Gliding over its surface, they rose to the summit, ascending, and disappearing amid the shoreless Heavens.

At last the Sun rose from behind the mount and the enchanting vision vanished.

On the third day, I came across three intersections.

At the fifth crossroad, an emerald babbling brook was rolling down one of the pathways with white ripples. I followed along it.

Around noon, I reached the sixth crossing: where once again I was faced with three choices. One of trails passed by the statuesque mountain, which seemed to be guarding this path. I chose it without hesitation.

When I came to my seventh intersection, which also featured three trails, I followed the one that was more strongly illumined by the rays of the Sun.

I was not alone, for I felt and realized that everything around me, each in its own unique ways, was offering praises to the Eternal Creator.

By evening, I caught the first sound flying towards me. Soon, on the slope of the mountain, to the right, I spied a dwelling, illumined by the last rays of the setting Sun. I headed towards it. It was built of stone. After giving thanks to the Creator for providing me with shelter, I serenely fell asleep.

At dawn I was awakened by voices. Two people stood before me, speaking in an unfamiliar tongue. But strangely enough, through some inner feeling, I was able to understand them and they me.

They asked whether I had a need for food. I answered: "I do, but only for spiritual food."

I went with them. They took me to a settlement, where I stayed for some time. The locals conversed with me a lot, and I was entrusted with a number of tasks and activities, which I carried out with the greatest satisfaction.

Then I was led further; I was told that the time had come for this.

At another place I was welcomed like a dear member of the family, and then again, when the time arrived, I was led further and further.

I lost track of time, for I did not think about it. Each day brought me something new, surprisingly wise and wonderful. And sometimes it seemed to me that everything that I was experiencing and that was happening to me, was a wondrous waking dream, for which I could find no explanation.

Thus time passed. Finally, I was told that the time had come for me to return home and that my path would lie through Constantinople.

For the time being, the human mind is unable to grasp what I saw there and what I learnt. Yet the day for this knowledge will come as well — and in due time the Lord will reveal to the worthiest ones incomparably more than to me.

As I leave this world, I shall relate what is possible.

The Country of Belovodye is not a fairy tale, but reality. It is called differently in different peoples' legends. The marvellous abodes there are home to radiant, gentle, humble, patient, compassionate, merciful, and insightful Great Sages — the Colleagues of the

Supreme World, wherein the Spirit of God dwells, as in His own Temple. These Great Saintly Devotees, uniting with the Lord, indeed constitute with Him the one Spirit. They toil tirelessly by the sweat of their brows, together with all the Heavenly Forces of Light, for the good and the benefit of all peoples of the Earth.

This is where one finds the Kingdom of Pure Spirit, along with beauty, wondrous fires, elevated enchanting mysteries, joy, light, love, a special tranquillity, and unfathomable majesty.

Multitudes of people from every part of the globe aspire to discover this Secret Land. But only seven in every hundred years are invited to enter it. Out of them, six come back, taking with them the secret knowledge, the development of new senses, the radiance of the soul and the heart — just like me. And only one remains.

Those who stay there live as much they want and have as much they need. For them, time has stopped.

Whatever is happening in the world — everything is known there, everything is seen, everything is heard. When my spirit grew stronger, I was granted the opportunity to visit, outside the body, the highest mountain, also Constantinople, Kiev, as well as to know, see, and hear whatever I desired.

It is known there for sure that the Christian faith is the best for the Grand Prince and for all the people of our country. There is no faith more spiritual, grander, purer, brighter, or more beautiful. It alone is destined to unite the peoples of our country and to be indivisible with them.

For a thousand years, the forces of hell will attack relentlessly with frenzied fury and rage and shake our Kievan Rus to its very foundations. The more terrible the pressure, the stronger the faith welding our people together — and nothing will obstruct their path towards the Most High. The Forces of Pure Light and Ethereal Fire will defeat all foes. The Living Fires will heal the wounds of our happy country. On the ruins of the old, the Great People, rich in the beauty of the spirit, will revive. The best of the chosen ones will bring the Word of the Living God to all countries of the Earth. They will give peace to the world, grace to humanity, and open the Gates of Life of the Future Age.

HISTORICAL
BACKGROUND

During the 10th-century reign of Prince Igor (from 912 to 945), the son of Rurik, the Christian cathedral church of St. Elias already existed in Kiev.

The wife of Prince Igor, Grand Princess Olga (a regent of Kievan Rus for her son Sviatoslav from 945 until 960), after being baptized, began taking steps to spread Christianity.

According to the narratives of the chroniclers, the grandson of Olga, Grand Prince Vladimir (reigned from 980 to 1015), spent a long time researching the question of which religion to adopt. In 986, he negotiated with the Volga Bulgarians (Mohammedans), the Khazars of the Jewish faith, the Germans (or Western Christians), and the Greek sage Cyril.

The dispatch of the embassy to Belovodye, on the basis of this historical data, could have taken place in the spring of 987. The baptism of Grand Prince Vladimir and Kievan Rus occurred in 988. According to the narrative, the death of Father Sergius can be attributed to the year 1043 — during the reign of Yaroslav the Wise (987 + 56 = 1043).

V.G.
1893

THANK YOU!

If you enjoyed this book, please consider leaving a review, even if it is only a line or two. It would make all the difference and would be very much appreciated.

In 1925, in many newspapers worldwide, an extensive article by the Mongolian explorer, Dr. Lao Chin, appeared, telling of his journey to the Valley of Shambhala. He was forbidden to write about the wondrous spiritual phenomena there. However, Dr. Lao Chin mentioned that the valley's inhabitants lived for many centuries but looked like middle-aged people, and they were characterized by clairvoyance, telepathy, and other higher abilities. Among other things, he saw how they levitated and even became invisible to the physical eye.

If you are interested in reading Dr. Lao Chin's article about his visit to one of the Abodes of Shambhala, please sign up for our newsletter here:

radiantbooks.co/bonus

OTHER TITLES PUBLISHED BY RADIANT BOOKS

The Land of the Gods
by H. P. Blavatsky

Blavatsky's long-hidden story is a beautifully written account of an exceptional journey into Shambhala and a profound introduction to the ancient wisdom tradition, which once was known to all but became available only to a few.

The Mystery of Christ
by Thales of Argos

Eye-opening and heart-touching, *The Mystery of Christ* brings a fresh perspective, an uncommon insight, and spiritual depth to the dramatic events which occurred two thousand years ago.